DIALO[G]UE

BETWEE[N]

A PRI[EST]

AND A

DYING MAN

BY

MARQUIS DE SADE

*From an
Unpublished Manuscript Edited
With an Introduction
And Notes by*
MAURICE HEINE
Translated by
SAMUEL PUTNAM

CHICAGO
PASCAL COVICI, *Publisher*
MCMXXVII

*Of this edition there have been printed for
Pascal Covici in May 1927, by The Cuneo Press, Inc.,
six hundred and fifty numbered copies only
on French hand-made paper and the
type distributed. Typography by
Douglas C. McMurtrie
This is No. 6 68*

TO

JEAN PAULHAN

IN FRIENDLY TRIBUTE

M. H.

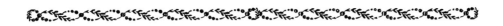

FOREWORD

The Atheist is the man of nature — SYLVAIN MARÉCHAL

I

"I SHOULD LIKE to be able to cite M. de Sade; he has more than enough mind, reasoning power and erudition; but his infamous romances of *Justine* and *Juliette* have caused him to be rejected from a sect where only virtue is spoken of."

Thus, in 1805, at the end of his second supplement to the *Dictionnaire des Athées,* did the illustrious astronomer Joseph-Jérôme Le Français de La Lande express himself.

It may be that the good man was merely being careful not to displease his colleague of the Institute, that Buonaparte whom Sylvain Maréchal rashly had included, five years before, in his *Dictionnaire des Athées Anciens et Modernes,* and who had later become the Lord's anointed. However this may be, Napoleon found himself upon the throne, and the Marquis de Sade was at Charenton: there was, therefore, no lack of courage in thus recognizing in a prisoner the power of reason, the exercise of which reasons of state had denied him.

The objection of La Lande would, nevertheless, have appeared a specious one to any philosophic mind. Had not the Baron d'Holbach foreseen and refuted just such an objection, in his *Système de la Nature,* (London, 1770, octavo, Vol. II, Ch. xiii, p. 372?)

"At sight of a work filled with verities, we are not embarrassed by the manners of the workman. What difference does it make to the universe whether Newton was sober or intemperate, chaste or a *débauché?* The only thing that concerns us is to know whether or not he has reasoned well, whether or not his principles are sure, whether or not the parts of his system hang together, whether or not his work contains more demonstrated truths than it does hazarded ideas. In the same manner, judge of the principles of an Atheist. . . ."

Undoubtedly. But at the dawn of the nineteenth century, atheism had become a virtuous sect, and the members of that sect would have felt a reproach in sharing the indulgence of their master.

Moreover, the men who then made a profession of atheistic faith—and these words are not juxtaposed without intention—were, for the most part, old men. They belonged to that eighteenth century, of which they were, in a manner, the testamentary executors. It is Sylvain Maréchal himself in his *Discours Préliminaire, ou Réponse à la Demande: qu'est-ce qu'un Athée?* whom we find, in the year 1800, placing his work under the auspices of the philosophic century.

"It was not necessary," he exclaims, "for the last year of the eighteenth century, that century which is so memorable, to elapse, before one dared to publish, at last, what all sane minds were thinking and keeping to themselves. . . ."

But what sort of atheism was it that these atheists professed?

If atheism has had representatives in all lands and ages known to human society, then its doctrine and its expression should have remained invariable. There is no doubt that the modern atheist, fed on the most recent physico-chemical conceptions of matter, is nearer to the mediæval atheist, who turned alchemist, than he is to the atheist of the eighteenth century.

"What, in short, is an Atheist? He is a man who destroys chimeras which are harmful to the human race, in order to lead men back to nature, to experience and to reason. He is a thinker who, having meditated upon matter, its energy, its properties and its modes of activity, has no need, in explaining the phenomena of the universe and the operations of nature, to conceive of ideal powers, imaginary intelligences and reasoning beings which, far from making nature better understood, render her capricious, inexplicable, unknowable and futile, so far as the happiness of human beings is concerned."

This definition, taken from the Baron d'Holbach (*Op. cit.,* Vol. II, Ch. xi, p. 323) may be looked upon as one of the clearest and most explicit which his age has furnished. But do these obvious negations achieve anything beyond a sentimental conception of a Nature useful to men and preoccupied with their happiness? And a few pages further on, do we not hear, monotonous as a litany, certain invocations, under other names, to those same "ideal powers," those same "imaginary intelligences," so energetically reproved above?

"O Nature! Sovereign of all beings! And you, her adorable daughters, virtue, reason, truth! Be ye always our sole divinities; it is you who should receive the incense and the homage of the earth." (*Op. cit.,* Vol. II, Ch. xiv, p. 411.)

II

THIS atheistic mythology might well, on one side or another, attach itself to the "natural philosophy" set forth in the *Discours Préliminaire* to the *Encyclopédie:* it would not too greatly have put out the academic philosophers. In the works published under their names, Diderot and Alembert display little sympathy for that atheism of which they suspected their dangerous adversaries, or for atheists themselves, those vexatious fellows whose brutal frankness ran the risk of compromising everything. What, then, did atheism mean to the Encyclopædists? In an article taken from the private papers of M. Formey, secretary of the Royal Academy of Prussia, that ancient shepherd gives us the following definition:

"It is the opinion of those who deny the existence of a God who is the creator of the world. Thus, a simple ignorance of God would not constitute atheism. In order to be laden with the odious brand of atheism, one must have had the notion of God and have rejected it. A state of doubt is not, any the more, formal atheism.... We are thus led to treat as atheists only those who declare openly that they have taken sides regarding the dogma of the existence of God and that they sustain the negative. . . . Atheism does not limit itself to deforming the idea of God, but destroys that idea entirely."

Although the meshes of this casuistry were sufficiently slack to permit a goodly number of atheists to escape, there were those who refused the means of flight thus proffered them, and who ended by proclaiming what they were. What was to be done with them? Oh, philosophy abandoned them; worse yet, it pronounced their condemnation and demanded their execution. . . .

"The most tolerant man will not controvert the point that the magistrate has the right to put down all those who dare to profess atheism, and even to cause them to perish, if he cannot otherwise deliver society from their presence. . . . If he may punish those who do a wrong to a single person, he has, undoubtedly, an equal right to punish those who do a wrong to all society, by denying that there is a God. . . . A man of this sort may be looked upon as an enemy of all others, since he overthrows all the foundations upon which the conservation and the felicity of the others are in principle established. Such a man might be punished by any one, by right of natural law."

When we find the *Encyclopédie* (1751, folio edition, Vol. I, pp. 815 et seq.) pronouncing such a verdict, shall we blame the circumspect reservations of a La Mettrie or the honorable amends of an Helvetius, after the condemnation of his book, *De l'Esprit?* Each had reason to fear the decrees of "natural law," as executed by their friends, at least as much as they did the thunderbolts of parliament, aimed by their adversaries. It is not without reason that Sylvain Maréchal, hailing the birth of the nineteenth century (*Dictionnaire des Athées,* Paris, An VIII, p. lxix,) calls our attention to "how servile and routine-ridden, despite all its enlightenment and pretentions, despite its liberal ideas and its impudences, the eighteenth century still was."

III

THIS harsh judgment would remain without appeal, if the Marquis de Sade had not lived, or if his work, persecuted like his person, had not in part escaped the rage of the destroyers. Twelve consecutive years of arbitrary detention † were employed by him in devouring the writings of the philosophers, the historians and the romancers: a vast amount of labor in the way of documentation and of editing was the result of the leisure accorded him by the "kindness of the king," and the results were to be shown when, thanks to the liberty given him by the Revolution, he launched, against the débris of a society which had oppressed him, the explosive pages of the *Philosophie dans le Boudoir,* of the *Nouvelle Justine* and of *Juliette.* It was in these works that he developed, quite at his ease, his atheism, and if he has not entirely rejected the prevalent conceptions of his century, if he still invokes na-

---

†"Here [Paris, 1776] his vicious practices became notorious, and in 1772 he was condemned to death at Aix for an unnatural offense, and for poisoning. He fled to Italy, but in 1777 he was arrested in Paris, removed to Aix for trial, and there found guilty. In 1778 he escaped from prison, but was soon re-arrested and finally committed to the Bastille. Here he began to write plays and obscene novels. In 1789 he was removed to the Charenton Lunatic Asylum, but was discharged in 1790, only to be recommitted as incurable in 1803. He died there on the 2nd of December, 1814."—*Encyclopædia Britannica.*

ture as a personality, it is not the amiable philanthropic goddess of the *Système de la Nature,* who no longer finds any grace in the presence of Voltaire; it is, rather, the catastrophic divinity who haunts the crater of Mount Aetna.

"The more I seek to surprise her secrets"—thus speaks the chemist, Almani—"the more I behold her solely working for the harm of men. Follow her in all her operations; you will never find her other than voracious, destructive and mischievous, never other than inconsistent, contrary and devastating. ... Should one not be right in saying that her murderous art has for object only the creation of new victims, that evil is her single element, and that it is only to cover the earth with blood, with tears and with grief that she has been endowed with the creative faculty, that it is only to let loose plagues that she employs her energies? One of your modern philosophers has declared himself the lover of nature; ah well, as for me, my friend, I declare myself her executioner. Study her, follow her, this atrocious nature, and you will see her create only to destroy, never arriving at her ends except by murders and, like the minotaur, fattening herself only on the misfortunes and the destruction of men." (*La Nouvelle Justine* Vol. III, p. 62.)

The point should not be lost sight of that De Sade is an absolutist; that he always follows his thought straight out to the end, to the extreme limit of its logical consequences. That these consequences may overthrow popular prejudices, accepted ideas, social conventions, moral laws — all this is no concern of his. He not merely states in writing, whenever the opportunity presents itself, that God is not, he constantly thinks it and acts in accordance with the thought; and this proud and unshakable certitude is, certainly, the sin humanity has found it hardest to forgive in him. But it is here that he reaches the heights, and his imprecations attain the validity of prayers:

"O thou!" he exclaims, "who hast created all that exists in the world; thou, of whom I do not possess the least idea; thou, whom I only know upon hearsay and from what my fellow men, who every day are the victims of their own snares, have told me; bizarre and fantastic being who art called God, I here, formally, authentically and publicly declare that I never have possessed the least faith in thee, and this for the excellent reason that I have found nothing that could persuade me of an absurd entity the reality of which nothing in the world attests. If I am wrong, and if, when I no longer exist, thou shouldst come to prove to me my error—if (which is against all the laws of verisimilitude and of reason) thou shouldst come to convince me of thine existence, so strongly denied by me now, what then? Thou wouldst render me either happy or unhappy. In the former case, I should acknowledge and cherish thee; in the latter case, I should abhor thee: then, since it is clear that no reasonable man could indulge in any such calculation as this, how, with that power which should be the first of thine attributes if thou dost exist—how canst thou leave man with an alternative so insulting to thy glory?" (*Histoire de Juliette,* Vol. II, p. 318.)

Atheism, in a man of this stamp, could not clothe itself in very amiable forms, and it is easy to conceive why the peaceable La Lande recoiled when the moment came to place such a one in his pantheon. Not only is the anarchy of De Sade incommensurate with the grandeurs of astronomy, but his conception of man is enough to splinter the vaults of all the temples.

IV

NOR is it necessary to seek among redoubtable and unknown enemies the motives of so prudent an ostracism directed against the most rigorous of atheists. The fundamental vice which the virtuous telescope of La Lande was able to discover in the writings of De Sade was the deliberately anti-Christian and habitually blasphemous character of his work. To take exception to the existence of God, to deny it theoretically, from the abstract and metaphysical point of view, remaining all the while a respecter of current morality, even in its religious manifestations, proving by one's acts that a respectable man, even though he were an atheist, knew better than to depart from such a code in practice—such was, necessarily, the social attitude of atheists worthy of finding a place in the *Dictionnaire.* La Lande himself does not fail to exhibit a controversial courtesy toward the pope, when the latter comes to Paris to crown the emperor.

"The pope said to me, on the 13th of December, 1804, that he did not understand how so great an astronomer as I could be an atheist. I replied to him that metaphysical opinions had nothing to do with

[18]

the respect due to religion; that such a respect was necessary, even though the church were no more than a political establishment; that I saw to it that religion was respected in my house, and that my curate came there to find succour for the poor; that I had this year caused the little ones of my household to make their first communion; that I had indulged in great praises of the Jesuits; that I had distributed holy bread in my parish; and I also spoke to him of other things." (Second Supplement to the *Dictionnaire des Athées,* by Jérôme de La Lande, 1805, octavo, p. 88.)

Let us see, now, how Juliette relates her fabled interview with Pius VI:

"'Proud phantom,' I replied to this old despot, 'the habit you have of deceiving men leads you to endeavor to deceive yourself. . . . There comes out of Galilee a religion the foundation-stones of which are: poverty, equality and a hatred of the rich. . . . It is forbidden the disciples of this cult ever to make any provision for themselves. . . . The first apostles of this religion gained their bread by the sweat of their brows. . . . Well enough; I now ask you what relation there is between those first institutions and the immense riches which you have gathered for yourself in Italy. Is it to the Gospel or the robberies of your predecessors that you owe so much property? . . . . Ah! if only all the peoples might undeceive themselves at once on the score of those papal idols which, down to the present time, have brought them nothing but indigence and misfortune! If only all the peoples of the earth, groaning under the results produced by centuries of wickedness like this, would unite to dethrone their tyrant and to cast down, at the same time, the stupid and barbarous, the idolatrous, sanguinary and impious religion which, for an instant, could think of accepting or of setting up such a tyrant.'" (*Histoire de Juliette,* Vol. IV, pp. 269-284.)

And when Brisa-Testa is admitted, at Stockholm, into the *Loge du Nord,* what vow is it that he there pronounces?

"I swear to exterminate all the kings of the earth; to wage eternal warfare on the Catholic religion and on the pope; to preach the liberty of peoples, and to found a universal republic." (*Op. cit.,* Vol. V, p. 119.)

In the mouth of Dolmancé, anti-Christianity is not so much a consequence of atheism as an argument in its favor. This entire passage, from the third dialogue of the *Philosophie dans le Boudoir,* being, as it is, in the nature of an energetic commentary on the "Dialogue Between a Priest and a Dying Man," should be quoted:

"That deific chimera of yours, does it clear up anything? I defy any one to prove it to me. Supposing I do deceive myself regarding the inherent properties of matter, I, at least, face but one difficulty. What do you do, in offering me your God? You merely give me one difficulty the more. And how can you ask me to admit as the cause of something I do not understand something that I understand still less? Is it by means of the dogmas of the Christian religion that I am to examine . . . . that I am to picture to myself your frightful God? Look, then, at the picture I behold. . . . What do I see in the God of that infamous religion if not an inconsistent and barbarous being, creating today a world the construction of which he repents tomorrow? What do I see but a weak being, who never can make man take the course He wishes? . . . . But, you will reply to that, if he had created him in any other fashion, man would possess no merit. What a platitude! And what necessity is there for man to possess merit in the sight of his God? If he had been created wholly good, he never would have been able to commit evil, and in such a case, only, would the work be worthy of a god. To leave man a choice is to tempt him. Now God, in his infinite wisdom, knew well enough what the result would be. From that moment, he damns, at His own good pleasure, the creature that He Himself has created. What a horrible God is that! What a monster! What wickedness is more worthy of our hatred and of our implacable vengeance! . . . . Have no doubt on one point: at its very birth, this unworthy religion would have been destroyed without shift, if only there had been employed against it no other arms than the contempt it deserves; but it was persecuted; and so, it grew: that was inevitable. If, today, the effort were made to cover it with ridicule, it would soon fall. The adroit Voltaire never employed any other arms; and he is, of all writers, the one who may flatter himself with having made the greatest number of proselytes."

It is, again, Christianity which the pamphlet, *Français, encore un effort si vous voulez être républicains,* read by the chevalier in the fifth dialogue of the *Philosophie dans le Boudoir,* begins by attacking:

"If, unfortunately for him, the Frenchman were once more to bury himself alive in the darkness of Christianity, then, on the one hand, the pride, tyranny and despotism of the priests—vices constantly reborn in that impure horde—and, on the other hand, the baseness, the narrow views, the platitudinous dogmas and mysteries of that unworthy and fabled religion, blunting the pride of the republican soul, would soon lead him back under the yoke which his energy had just broken! Never lose sight of the fact that this puerile religion was one of the most effective arms in the hands of our tyrants; one of its first dogmas was *to render unto Caesar the things that are Caesar's* but we have dethroned Cæsar, and we are no longer willing to pay him anything. . . . Before ten years, by means of the Christian religion, with its superstition and its prejudices, your priests, despite their vows and their poverty, would resume once more over your souls that sway which they had usurped; they would enchain you once more to your kings, for the reason that the power of the latter is always a prop to them, and your republican edifice would tumble for lack of foundation. . . . Annihilate, then, forever, everything which may destroy your work. Remember that, the fruit of your labors being reserved for your posterity, it is your bounden duty to leave to the latter none of those dangerous germs which may plunge them back into that chaos from which you yourselves have had so much difficulty in escaping. Already, our prejudices are being dissipated; already, the people are abjuring the absurdities of Catholicism; they have already suppressed the temples and overthrown the idols; it is agreed that marriage is no more than a civil act; the confessionals, shattered, now serve as public firesides; the faithful pretenders, deserting the apostolic banquet, are leaving the god of flour to the mice. Frenchmen, do not stop here: all Europe, one hand upon the bandage that blinds her eyes, awaits on your part the effort which will snatch it from her brow. Make haste. . . . It is no longer at the knees of an imaginary being nor at those of a vile impostor that a republican ought to kneel; his only gods now should be *courage* and liberty. Rome disappeared as soon as Christianity began to be preached, and France is lost if she dreams of it more. One has but to examine, attentively, the absurd dogmas, the frightful mysteries, the monstrous ceremonies and the impossible morality of this disgusting religion, and one will see whether or not it is suited to a republic."

Of what use to multiply quotations? Without insisting upon their prophetic sense, we believe that enough have been given to distinguish, in its political and social roots, the atheism professed by De Sade from that atheism of which his contemporaries have transmitted to us the timorous expression.

V

THE little work of the Marquis de Sade which we here publish for the first time is possessed of a double interest for the curious: it is, of his literary works at present known, the earliest of those that we are able to date with certitude (1782), as well as the only one written in the same dialogue form as the *Philosophie dans le Boudoir*. It is generally known that the original edition of the latter bears the date of 1795: the absence of any manuscript renders uncertain the date at which it was first written. Between these two works, there has been little appreciable change except in political systems: in the interval, the Revolution has made a citizen of the marquis. Here, however, it is well not to be deceived: the patriotic and royalist tirade of the dying man and the republican and anarchistic proclamation of the chevalier may represent at bottom — *mutatis mutandis* — but one and the same oratorical precaution. It is, as a matter of fact, not so much politics that is treated in these two essays as metaphysics and morality, and particularly, atheism and the philosophy of eroticism. But this latter theme, which constitutes the sole burden of the "Philosophy" is barely indicated in the "Dialogue" now under consideration.

The unpublished manuscript from which we obtain the text of the "Dialogue Between a Priest and a Dying Man" is in the form of a brochure with a cover, consisting of twenty-three uncut sheets of blue laid paper, covered on both sides with the handwriting (so personal in character) of the Marquis de Sade. It consisted originally of twenty-four sheets, that is, of six sheets of foolscap size, folded in quarto form and bound into a single booklet, measuring approximately six by eight inches. But the first page is missing, having been detached by some one's tearing it away from the last, as is evident from the indentations of the paper and the relative position of the watermark.

In its present state, it was met with a number of times in the public sales of Paris, after the 31st of January, 1850, at which time it was knocked down, upon the decease of M. Villenave, a man of letters, for the ridiculous sum of 3 fr. 25. It reappeared almost at once, on the 25th of March, 1851, at the sale of the library of M. de C***. Finally, we find it catalogued in the collection of Mme. D***, disposed of at the Hôtel Drouot on the 6th of November, 1920.

The *Sujet de Zélonide, comédie en cinq actes et en vers libres,* begins on page three, the first page in the present state of the manuscript. Page ten is reserved for a *Suite du tableau des empereurs grecs,* a sort of historical résumé in two columns. Historical notes and reflections occupy page eleven and the top of page twelve, in the middle of which page the "Dialogue" begins. The latter continues, without interruption, down to the bottom of page twenty-four, the "Note" that ends it taking up the first five lines of page twenty-five. The remainder of the manuscript contains more historical notes and quotations, as well as literary criticisms and philosophic reflections, certain of which are remarkable. The forty-eighth and last page is entitled *Page de Brouillon* and is arranged, like page ten, in two columns.

At the bottom of page forty-seven, on the recto of the last sheet, there appears, in the outer margin, an important autograph notation: "Finished the 12th of July, 1782." It was, then, in the beginning of his forty-third year, at the end of the third year of his detention by warrant in the Château de Vincennes, that Donatien-Alphonse-François de Sade composed this work as we find it in his waste-book. The handwriting is firm and clear, with few erasures. The present edition respects the original text, except in case of an obvious *lapsus calami.*

VI

THE subject of the death of an atheist inspired, in the century of philosophy, only the sombre genius of De Sade. Sylvain Maréchal, the old swain, Sylvain, of the *Dictionnaire d'amour,* has composed a charming page on the same subject. Perhaps, we shall be able better to savour his amiable eloquence when it is placed beside the polemic bitterness of the "Dialogue:"

"Has he come to the end of his existence? If so, he masses all his forces to enjoy the pleasures that remain to him and then closes his eyes forever, but with the certainty that he is leaving a memory honorable and dear in the hearts of his neighbors, at whose hands he receives the last tokens of esteem and attachment. His rôle ended, he retires tranquilly from the stage, to make place for other actors, who shall take him for model. He experiences, without doubt, lively regrets at this separation from all that he has loved, but reason tells him that this is in accordance with the immutable order of things. Moreover, he knows that he does not wholly die. The father of a family is eternal; he returns new born in each of his children; and even down to the fragments of his body, nothing of him can be annihilated. An indestructible link in the great chain of being, the *man-without-God* embraces all infinity in his thought and is consoled by the reflection that death is but a displacement of matter and a change of form. At the moment of quitting life, he reviews in memory, if he has the leisure, the good that he has been able to do, as well as the faults he has committed. Proud of his existence, he has not bent the knee to any except the author of his days. He has walked upon the earth, head high and step firm, the equal of all other beings, having to give an account to no one, but only to his conscience. His life is as full as that of Nature: behold, there is a Man. (*Dictionnaire des Athées,* An VIII, pp. xxiii-xxv.)"

If we rely upon the touching testimony of his friend, La Lande, Maréchal was not guilty of the supreme madness of a death contrary to his vows. And De Sade himself, so different in character, must have given proof, in the presence of death, of an equally tranquil assurance.

MAURICE HEINE

DIALOGUE BETWEEN A PRIEST
AND A DYING MAN

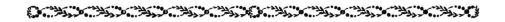

DIALOGUE BETWEEN A PRIEST
AND A DYING MAN

THE PRIEST

NOW that you 'have come to that fatal moment when the veil of illusion is rent only to permit straying man a sight of the cruel picture of his errors and his vices, do you not repent, my child, the many misdemeanors you have been led to commit through weakness and human fragility?

THE DYING MAN

Yes, my friend, I repent.

THE PRIEST

Ah, then, profit from that happy remorse by obtaining from Heaven, during the brief interval that remains to you, a general absolution of your sins, and remember that it is only through meditation on the most blessed Sacrament of penitence that it will be possible for you to obtain the gift of eternal life.

THE DYING MAN

I do not understand you, any more than you have understood me.

THE PRIEST
What!

THE DYING MAN
I told you that I repented.

THE PRIEST
I heard you.

THE DYING MAN
Yes, but without understanding.

THE PRIEST
What do you mean . . . . ?

THE DYING MAN
Just this. . . . Since I have been created by nature with very lively tastes, with very strong passions, and have been placed in this world for the sole purpose of giving myself over to, and satisfying, those tastes and passions, and since these consequences of my having been created are, merely, necessities in keeping with the first designs of nature, or, if you prefer, essential corollaries to her plans for me, the whole being in accordance with her own laws, I repent not having sufficiently recognized her omnipotence, and the only remorse I feel has to do with the mediocre employment I have made of those faculties (criminal according to you, wholly natural according to me) which she gave me

for her own service: I have, at times, resisted her, and for this I am penitent. Blinded by the absurdities of your doctrines, I have combatted, for the sake of those doctrines, the violence of those desires which I received by an inspiration a good deal more divine, and this I repent: I have reaped only flowers, when I might have gathered an ample harvest of fruits . . . . there you have the just cause of my regret; please do me the honor not to suppose there is any other cause.

THE PRIEST

Oh, where are those errors, those sophistries of yours, leading you? You impute to the thing created all the power of the Creator, and this unfortunate tendency, which leads you astray is, though you will not see it, simply the result of that corrupt Nature which you endow with omnipotence.

THE DYING MAN

My friend, it appears to me your dialectic is as false as your mind itself. I wish you would either reason more justly or leave me to die in peace. What do you mean by "creator," and what do you understand by "corrupt nature"?

THE PRIEST

The Creator is the master of the universe; it is He who has made everything, created everything, and who preserves everything, as the simple consequence of His omnipotence.

THE DYING MAN
He's quite a chap, upon my word! Ah, well, tell me, then, why it is that this fellow, who is so powerful, still has created, according to you, a Nature that is corrupt.

THE PRIEST
What merit would men have had, if God had not left them a free choice, and if they had not encountered, upon the earth, the possibility either of doing good or of avoiding evil?

THE DYING MAN
And so, that god of yours must do everything crosswise, solely for the purpose of tempting, or of proving, his creature? He did not know his own creature, then? He doubted the result?

THE PRIEST
He undoubtedly knew what the result would be, but He wished to leave man the merit of choice.

THE DYING MAN
Of what use was that, since he knew what the choice would be? Why, if he is all-powerful, as you say—why did he not keep man in the right path and force him to choose the good?

[36]

THE PRIEST

Who can fathom the immense and infinite wisdom of God towards man, and who can understand all that we behold?

THE DYING MAN

The one who simplifies things, my friend, the one, above all, who does not multiply causes in order to confuse effects the more. What need have you of a second difficulty, when you cannot explain the first; and since it is possible that Nature alone has done all that you attribute to your god, why must you go seeking a master for her? The cause of what you do not understand is, it may be, the simplest thing in the world. Perfect your physics, and you will understand Nature better; purify your reason, banish your prejudices, and you will have no need of that god of yours.

THE PRIEST

Poor fellow! I believe you are nothing more than a Socinian. I have arms to fight you, but I see clearly that you are an atheist, and since your heart refuses the infinite and authentic proofs we every day receive of the existence of the Creator, I have nothing more to say to you. One does not give light to a blind man.

THE DYING MAN

My friend, you must grant me one point: the blinder

of us is, surely the one who puts a bandage over his eyes, not the one who snatches the bandage away. You build up, you invent, you multiply; as for me, I destroy, I simplify. You pile error upon error, while I combat all errors. Which is the blinder of the two?

THE PRIEST

You have no belief whatever, then, in God?

THE DYING MAN

None. And for a very simple reason, namely, that it is utterly impossible for me to believe what I do not understand. Between comprehension and faith, there should be a direct relation; comprehension is the first food of faith: where there is no comprehension, faith is dead, and those who, in such a case, pretend to have faith, are self-impostors. I defy you, yourself, to believe in the god you preach to me—because you cannot demonstrate him to me, because the power is not in you to define him for me, because, in short, you do not understand him. And since you do not understand him, you are unable to furnish me with any reasonable argument. In a word, whatever is beyond the limits of the human mind is a chimera or a futility, and your god can be only one or the other of these things. In the former case, I should be a fool to believe in him;

in the latter, an imbecile. My friend, prove to me the inertia of matter, and I will grant you your creator; prove to me that Nature is not sufficient to herself, and I will permit you to assume that she must have a master. Until that time, look for nothing from me: I only yield to evidence, and I receive evidence only through my senses: where they stop, my faith is powerless. I believe in the sun because I see it; I conceive it to be the unifying center of all the inflammable material in Nature; its periodical revolution pleases, without astonishing, me. It is an operation of physics, as simple, possibly, as that of electricity, but one which it is not permitted us to understand. What need have I to go further? When you shall have built me a scaffolding for your god above all that, shall I be any the further along, and will it not require quite as much effort to understand the workman as to define the work? As a consequence, you do me no service by setting up your edifying chimera; you have troubled my mind, but you have not enlightened it, and I owe you nothing but hatred as compensation. Your god is a machine which you have manufactured to serve your own passions; it moves at their direction, but when it interferes with my own passions, grant me the right to overthrow it. And so, at the moment when my weakened soul has need of philosophic calm, please do not come to terrify it with your sophistries, which frighten without convincing, which irritate without improving. This soul, my friend, is what Nature has willed it should be, that is to say, the result of those organs and their needs which she has been pleased to create for me. And since she has equal need of virtues and of vices, when it has pleased her to impell me to the former, she has done so; when she would impel me to the latter, she does it by inspiring in me certain desires; and I, likewise, have surrendered to these. Do not seek beyond her laws for the sole cause of all human inconsistency; and in her laws, look for no other principles than her own volition and her own needs.

THE PRIEST

Then everything in the world is inevitable.

THE DYING MAN

Assuredly.

THE PRIEST

But if everything is inevitable, then everything must be regulated.

THE DYING MAN

Has any one denied that?

THE PRIEST

And what could regulate everything that is, except an all-powerful and all-wise hand?

THE DYING MAN

Is it necessary for powder to blaze when one touches fire to it?

THE PRIEST

Yes.

THE DYING MAN

And what wisdom do you find in that?

THE PRIEST

None.

THE DYING MAN

It is, then, possible that there are certain things which are necessary, without any wisdom being involved; and it follows that it is also possible for all things to derive from a first cause, without there being either reason or wisdom in that first cause.

THE PRIEST

What point are you trying to make?

THE DYING MAN

I am proving to you that everything may be as it is, and as you see it to be, without any wise and reasonable cause, and that natural results must have natural causes, without need of supposing unnatural ones, such as your god would be who, as you already have admitted, stands in need of explanation, without himself being able to furnish any: I would prove to you, as a consequence, that your god is good for nothing and absolutely useless; and since there is every evidence that what is useless is non-existent, I have need, in order to convince myself of the fact that your god is a chimera, of no other reasons than those furnished me by the certainty I possess of his futility.

THE PRIEST

If you are off on that foot, it seems to me there is little use in speaking to you of religion.

THE DYING MAN

Why not? Nothing amuses me like evidence of the excessive fanaticism and imbecility of which men can be guilty on this score; there are, for me, some mistakes so prodigious that the contemplation of them, however horrible the picture, is always interesting. Answer my questions frankly, and above all, banish egotism. If I were so weak as to permit myself to be taken in by those ridiculous beliefs of yours concerning the fabled existence of a being who makes religion necessary, under what form should you advise me to render him my tribute of worship? Would you have me adopt the dreams of Confucius rather than the absurdities of Brahma? Should I adore the great serpent of the Africans, the star of the Peruvians or Moses' god of armies? What sect of Mahomet would you have me join, or which of the Christian heresies would, in your eyes, be preferable? Look well to your answer.

THE PRIEST

Can there be any doubt about my answer?

THE DYING MAN

There you have the perfect egotist.

THE PRIEST

No. It is merely because I love you as much as I do myself that I advise you in accordance with what I believe.

THE DYING MAN

We must love ourselves very little if we listen to such errors.

THE PRIEST

Ah, who could be so blind as not to be convinced by the miracles of our divine Redeemer?

THE DYING MAN

One who sees in him only the most ordinary of all knaves and the shallowest of impostors.

THE PRIEST

Ye Gods! Who hear him, yet do not strike him dead!

THE DYING MAN

No, my friend, all is at peace, because that god of yours, whether divine impotence or divine reason, or all that you would have him be—though I do not for a moment admit his existence, except out of condescension toward you or, if you prefer, to lend myself the better to your narrow views—because, I say, that god, if he did exist, as you are foolish enough to believe, would never, to convince us of his existence, have adopted means so ridiculous as those your Jesus supposes.

THE PRIEST

And what of the prophets, the miracles, the martyrs—are they not all proof?

THE DYING MAN

How can you, logically, expect me to accept as proof all that which in itself stands in need of proof? For prophecy to be a proof, it would be necessary, first of all, for me to be absolutely certain the prophecy had been made; but all that being a matter of history, it can possess for me no greater validity than all the other facts recorded in history, three-fourths of which are very doubtful. If I add to this the more than likely possibility that these prophecies have been handed down to me by interested historians, I shall be, as you see, more than justified in my doubt. Who will assure me, moreover, that such prophecies have not been made after the fact, that they are not the result of the simplest wisdom, such as that which discerns a happy reign under a just king or the fact that there is frost in winter? And if all this is so, how can you expect prophecy, which itself has so much need of proof, to become a proof to me? As to your miracles, they impose on me no more than do your prophecies. All knaves have performed them, and all fools have believed them. In order to be persuaded of the truth of a miracle, I should have to be convinced that the event which you call a miracle was one absolutely contrary to the laws of Nature, for only such an event could pass for a miracle. And who knows the laws of Nature well enough to be able to affirm the precise point at which they cease to function? It requires only two things to win credit for a miracle: a mountebank and a number of silly women. Away with you, and never seek

[45]

any other origin than that for those miracles of yours. All the new sectarians have performed miracles, and, what is strangest of all, they have all found imbeciles to believe them. Your Jesus has done nothing more singular than did Apollonius of Tyana, and yet, no one has thought of taking the latter for a god. As to your martyrs, they are, assuredly, the weakest of all your arguments. To make a martyr requires only enthusiasm and resistance, and since the opposite side affords me as many examples as your own, I shall never feel myself sufficiently authorized to believe that one side is better than the other, but shall be inclined, rather, to look on both with pity. Ah! my friend, if that god you preach did exist, would he have any need of miracles, of martyrs or of prophecy in establishing his empire? And if, as you say, the heart of man were his work, would it not be the sanctuary which he would choose as the abiding place of his law? That just law —it would have to be just, coming from a just god— would be ineffaceably engraved in the hearts of all, from one end of the universe to the other, and all men, through the delicate organ of conscience, would be brought to think and act alike, by reason of the common worship paid to the god of their being. All would have but one fashion of loving, adoring and serving him; and it would be as impossible for them not to recognize such a god as it would be to resist the inner impulse to worship him. What, in place of this, do I behold in the world? As many gods as there are countries, as many manners of serving those gods as there are different heads or different imaginations. And this multiplicity of opinions, among which it is physically impossible for me to choose, is, you would tell me, the work of a just god? Away with you, preacher. You outrage your own god by presenting him to me in such a manner. Permit me to deny him wholly, for if he exists, then I shall outrage him less by my incredulity than do you with your blasphemies. Be reasonable, Mr. Preacher. Your Jesus is worth no more than Mahomet, Mahomet no more than Moses, and all three no more than Confucius, who enunciated a few good principles, while the three others are unreasonable in their teachings; but in general, all fellows of that sort are but impostors, whom the philosopher laughs at, whom the mob believes, and whom the magistrate ought to string up by the neck.

THE PRIEST

Alas! They did it only too well for one of the four.

THE DYING MAN

He was the one who best deserved it. He was seditious, rowdy, a slanderer, a knave, a libertine, a clown and a dangerous criminal; he possessed the art of imposing on the people, and he was, as a result, liable to punishment in a realm in the state Jerusalem was in at that time. They were, therefore, very wise in getting rid of him, and this is the only case in which my principles, very gentle and tolerant otherwise, would admit the severity of Themis. I excuse all errors except those which may become dangerous to the government under which one lives. The majesty of kings, alone, impresses me; kings are the only ones whom I respect, and the man who does not love his country and his king is not fit to live.

THE PRIEST

But you must admit there is something after this life. It is impossible that your mind should not sometimes have endeavored to pierce the thick shadows of the fate that awaits us. And what doctrine could be more satisfying than the one which provides an infinity of pains for the evil and an eternity of rewards for the good?

THE DYING MAN

How is that, my friend? The prospect of nothingness has never frightened me; I see in it only a consolation and something very simple. All the rest is the work of pride; there is reason only in this view. There is in nothingness nothing terrifying or absolute. Do I not have constantly under my eyes the example of the perpetual generative and regenerative work of nature? Nothing perishes, my friend; nothing in this world is destroyed: today, a man; tomorrow, a worm; the day after tomorrow, a fly—what is that, if not perpetual existence? And why would you have me rewarded for virtues when I can claim no merit in possessing them, or punished for crimes, when I am not the master of myself? Can you reconcile the goodness of your supposed god with such a doctrine, and could he have willed to create me merely to give himself the pleasure of punishing me, all as the consequence of a choice I have made when I was never free to choose.

THE PRIEST

But you are.

THE DYING MAN

Yes, according to your prejudiced view; but reason destroys such prejudices, and the doctrine of human liberty was never invented except to spawn that doctrine of divine grace which is so favorable to your reveries. What man is there in the world who, seeing the scaffold beside his proposed crime, would commit that crime, if he were free not to do so? We are led on by an irresistible force, and never for a moment are we sufficiently masters of ourselves to be able to choose any other course than the one to which we are impelled. There is not a single virtue that is not necessary to nature, and inversely, not a single needless crime, and it is in the perfect equilibrium which nature maintains between the two that all her science lies. But can we, by any possibility, be guilty because we fall in the direction she pushes us? No more guilty than is the wasp that comes to sink its sting in your flesh.

THE PRIEST

Then, the greatest of crimes should inspire no terror in us.

THE DYING MAN

That is not what I said. It is enough for the law to condemn and justice to punish; this is all that is needed to terrify and restrain us. But when, unfortunately, a crime has been committed, one should be wise enough to accept it and not to indulge in sterile remorse. Remorse is vain, since it can neither restrain us from crime nor repair a crime when it has been committed. It is, therefore, absurd to yield to remorse, and still more absurd to fear being punished in another world, if we are happy enough to have escaped punishment in this one. God forbid I should, by this, lend encouragement to crime. One, surely, should avoid doing this so far as one can, but it is through reason that crime is to be fled, and not through false fears, which lead to nothing, and which soon lose their effect in a soul possessed of any strength whatsoever. Reason, my friend—yes, reason alone should teach us that doing ill to our fellow men never can make us happy, while our hearts should tell us that to contribute to their felicity is the greatest privilege nature has given us upon this earth; all human morality is contained in this one precept: *to make others as happy as one would like to be one's self,* and never to do an ill to others that we should not want them to do to us. That, my friend, is the only principle we should follow, and there is need neither of religion nor of God in order to sense and admit such a code; all that is required is a good heart. . . . But I feel myself growing weaker, Mr. Preacher. Forsake your prejudices, be a man, be human. Without fear and without hope, leave your gods and your religions. All that they are good for is to put a sword in the hand of man, and the very mention of all these horrors has caused more blood to be spilled upon the earth than all the other wars and all the other scourges, put together. Renounce the idea of another world; there is none; but do not renounce the pleasure of happiness, and of creating happiness, in this world. That is the only means nature offers you of repeating and of prolonging your existence. My friend, pleasure has always been to me the dearest of blessings; I have swung incense before her all my life, and I have always desired to die in her arms. My end is approaching. Six women, more beautiful than day, are in the next room. I have been keeping them for this moment. Take your share of them, and, in accordance with my example, endeavor to forget, upon their bosoms, all the vain sophistries of superstition and all the imbecile errors of hypocrisy.

NOTE

[*The Dying Man rings, the women enter, and the Preacher becomes, in their arms, a man corrupted by nature, for not having been able to explain what corrupt nature was.*]

THE END

CPSIA information can be obtained at www.ICGtesting.com
Printed in the USA
BVOW050041030812

296893BV00017B/1/P